THE MESSAGE FROM JESUS CHRIST RETURN

RETURN, O ISRAEL

ANTHONY MWANGI

Crony Trading LTD

To Jesus Christ,
whose voice is the trumpet,
whose word shakes the heavens,
and who has personally sent this message
to His people — the Christians who are Israel
in this generation,
called to return, awaken, and make ready.

To the eternal Messenger and the Message,
the Faithful Witness,
the Lamb upon the throne,
the King who speaks still,
summoning His remnant from the four winds
with a voice like many waters.

To the Holy Spirit,
the Breath that carries the command,
the Fire that seals the Bride,
the Counsel who opens the ancient scrolls
and writes truth upon the heart.

To Israel — the scattered, the chosen, the rising,
from Africa to Zion to the islands of the sea.
May the lost tribes hear the sound,
may the sons return home,
and may the daughters rise in holy strength.

And to every reader who feels eternity trembling within you:
This message is for you.
This trumpet was sounded for your generation.
Stand, awaken, and behold the King.

Even so — come, Lord Jesus.

"Behold, I stand at the door, and knock." — *Revelation 3:20 (KJV)*

The King calls.
The nations stir.
Israel must return.

Even so, come, Lord Jesus.

SABBATH FIRE

To Jesus Christ,
whose voice is the trumpet,
whose word shakes the heavens,
and who has personally sent this message
to His people — the Christians who are Israel
in this generation,
called to return, awaken, and make ready.

To the eternal Messenger and the Message,
the Faithful Witness,
the Lamb upon the throne,
the King who speaks still,
summoning His remnant from the four winds
with a voice like many waters.

To the Holy Spirit,
the Breath that carries the command,
the Fire that seals the Bride,
the Counsel who opens the ancient scrolls
and writes truth upon the heart.

To Israel — the scattered, the chosen, the rising,
from Africa to Zion to the islands of the sea.
May the lost tribes hear the sound,
may the sons return home,
and may the daughters rise in holy strength.

And to every reader who feels eternity trembling within you:
This message is for you.
This trumpet was sounded for your generation.
Stand, awaken, and behold the King.

Even so — come, Lord Jesus.

"Behold, I stand at the door, and knock." — Revelation 3:20 (KJV)

The King calls.
The nations stir.
Israel must return.

Even so, come, Lord Jesus.

SABBATH FIRE

CONTENTS

FOREWORD

There are moments in history when heaven bends low,
when the breath of God presses upon the earth,
and the Spirit releases a sound that refuses to be ignored.
We are living in such an hour.

The message contained in these pages is not born of human imagination,
nor shaped by the ambitions of men.
It is a *summons* — a divine call sent forth from the throne of Jesus Christ,
the One whose voice is the trumpet,
whose eyes read the ages,
whose footsteps already echo upon the mountains.

The world is trembling under converging signs.
Nations shake, kingdoms crumble, and systems once thought immovable
are being weighed in the balances of truth.
Yet in the midst of this shaking,
a different sound rises:
the cry of the Spirit calling the true Israel
the people of covenant,
the remnant in every land,
the scattered seed of faith to return.

This book carries that sound.

It speaks to our generation with clarity and fire,
unveiling ancient precepts with fresh urgency,

and reminding us that the King is not a distant hope
He is at the door.

The prophetic insights here are not merely teachings;
they are instructions for readiness.
They strengthen the soul, awaken the spirit,
and call the body to stand in holiness
as living stones of His emerging temple.

What you hold is a witness.
A horn blown across the continents.
A banner lifted to the nations.
A reminder that Jesus Christ is both Messenger and Message and
He is speaking now.

My prayer is simple:
May your heart burn as you read.
May your eyes open to the hour.
May the Spirit draw you into alignment with heaven's decree.

And may every word prepare you to echo the cry of the Bride:
"Even so, come, Lord Jesus."

— Foreword
"He that hath an ear, let him hear what the Spirit saith unto the churches."

INTRODUCTION

This book is not an accident of study, nor the product of human strategy.
It is a message delivered
spoken, revealed, impressed, and ordered by the Lord Jesus Christ Himself.

Every Scripture you will encounter in these pages was not selected by tradition, convenience, or opinion.
They were **given**,
one upon another,
precept upon precept,
line upon line,
exactly as the Lord instructed His servant.

The arrangement is intentional.
The order is divine.
The message is urgent.

In an age where noise fills the spiritual atmosphere and countless voices compete for attention, this work stands apart for one reason alone:
its source is Christ.

Not Christ imagined.
Not Christ interpreted through culture.
But Christ —
the risen Son of God,
the faithful and true Witness,
the One who walks among the candlesticks

and speaks with a voice like many waters.

His call is simple, but uncompromising:
Return, O Israel.

Not the Israel defined solely by borders and history,
but the Israel defined by covenant
those who hear His voice,
those sealed by His Spirit,
those who belong to Him in this generation.

The purpose of this book is not merely to inform;
it is to transform.
It is designed to turn hearts back to the Lord,
to awaken the sleeping,
to steady the faithful,
and to prepare the remnant for the nearness of His return.

We stand in the shadow of the final hour.
Prophecies once distant now march across the headlines.
The earth groans.
Nations tremble.
And the Spirit speaks the same message Christ spoke in the days of
the prophets:

Hear, O heavens.
Give ear, O earth.
My people have forgotten their God.
Return.

As you begin reading, approach these pages with a listening heart.
Not to the voice of a writer,
nor the echo of a teacher,
but to the One who authored the beginning
and will soon appear in glory.

This is His message.
His timing.
His calling.

And blessed is the one who hears it and returns.

Even so, Lord Jesus… come quickly.

PREFACE

This book stands as a strategic communiqué—an executive briefing from the King of Kings to His covenant people. It is not merely a compilation of insights, nor a creative reconstruction of ancient themes. It is, in truth, a message sourced from one place only: **the voice of Jesus Christ Himself**.

The words, the scriptures, the order, the cadence—they were not selected by preference or arranged by convenience. They came exactly as they were given. This text exists because the Lord chose to speak, and because a servant chose to listen.

In a world operating at break-neck velocity, where spiritual noise often drowns out spiritual clarity, Jesus Christ issues a directive designed to recalibrate His people and realign them with their original covenant identity. His call is simple, yet seismic: **Return, O Israel**. Return to your name, your purpose, your inheritance, and your God.

The message carried within these pages is not theoretical. It is actionable. It is a rollout plan for spiritual restoration, a blueprint for covenant reinstatement, and a Kingdom-level change management strategy authored by Christ Himself.

Its purpose is to prompt movement; internal transformation, external alignment, corporate awakening. It invites every reader into a forward-leaning posture, ready to respond to the same voice that thundered on Sinai and now whispers through the Spirit.

This preface is only the threshold. The true weight rests in the message that follows. And the message is His. Entirely His.

With humility, I simply deliver what was entrusted.

**For the glory of Jesus Christ,
and for the return of His people.**

PROLOGUE

The Trumpet of His Return

The trumpet of the Lord trembles upon the winds, shaking the silence of the earth.
A sound older than creation rises again; the decree of Heaven thunders through the veil: *the time is short.*

The Son of Man stands at the threshold of glory, His countenance like the sun in its strength, His eyes as flames of living fire. From His hands, light pours forth; the eternal testimony of love and judgment. He looks upon the nations, and nothing is hidden. The proud are weighed, the wicked exposed, and the faithful quickened with holy fear.

His voice rolls through the heavens: "Return unto Me, O Israel even My true Church, My covenant seed, My remnant of Spirit and truth. For I come quickly, and My reward is with Me."

The cry of the Spirit echoes through cities and wilderness alike: *"Awake, O Zion! Clothe thyself in holiness; put on thy beautiful garments, for thy King approacheth swiftly!"*
This is no lullaby for the complacent, no murmur for those who slumber in religion.
It is the roar of awakening, the trumpet of separation.

For the hour has come when judgment must begin at the house of God. The altars of compromise will be overturned; the lamps without oil will be found wanting.
Yet those who know His name, who bear His mark in their hearts, shall rise in radiant peace. They are His Israel; the temple

not made with hands, standing clothed in white, awaiting the cry, *"Behold, the Bridegroom cometh!"*

Even so, come, Lord Jesus.
Let the winds carry the last sound of grace before the fire descends.

CHAPTER 1

*The Cry of the Father: "Hear, O
Heavens"
(Isaiah 1:2–4 KJV)*

"Hear, O heavens, and give ear, O earth: for the LORD hath spoken, I have nourished and brought up children, and they have rebelled against me."

The courtroom of eternity opens, and the Judge of all creation speaks. Heaven and earth stand as witnesses; not silent, but trembling. From the dawn of time, the Father has watched His creation rise in glory and fall in pride. He nourished them with His Word, clothed them with His Spirit, and crowned them with His likeness, yet they turned from the fountain of living waters to carve cisterns that hold no life.

The grief of God is not the rage of a tyrant; it is the cry of a Father whose house lies empty. His voice reverberates through the generations:

"The ox knoweth his owner, and the ass his master's crib;

but Israel doth not know, My people doth not consider."

He compares His chosen to beasts, not in insult but in contrast; even creation obeys its Maker's rhythm, yet man, made in divine image, has forgotten his song.

1. Spiritology — The Wound in the Father's Heart

Rebellion is not first an act, but a breach of spirit. It is the silent divorce between breath and obedience, when sons forget the voice that formed them. The Spirit of the Lord hovers still, yearning to restore the connection. But many have traded revelation for religion, presence for performance, intimacy for image. The heavens are summoned because rebellion begins in the spirit-realm when light resists its own Source.

2. Soulogy — The Disease of Forgetfulness

The Father's cry exposes a fractured soul. Israel had memory without relationship; law without love. The mind retained the rituals, but the heart wandered to idols of comfort and pride. This is the wound of the modern believer: to know about God but not *know* Him,
to serve His name but not *bear* His nature.
The soul, untethered from Spirit, becomes a city without walls; defenceless against every whisper of deception.

3. Physiology — The Manifestation in the Body

The rebellion of spirit and soul manifests in the body.
When man disconnects from divine order, even the earth groans. Diseases multiply, systems decay, creation itself becomes witness against its stewards. The polluted land mirrors the polluted heart; what is unclean in the spirit reproduces corruption in the soil. The Father's grief is not abstract; it is embodied in drought, famine, and war. These are not punishments alone, but symptoms; signs

that man has left his covering.

4. Theology — The Covenant Broken and Renewed

Every covenant begins with *"I will be their God, and they shall be My people."* When Israel broke faith, the Father did not withdraw His mercy: He revealed His plan. Through prophets, He declared that restoration would come not by the sacrifice of bulls, but by the Lamb slain from the foundation of the world. Thus the cry, "Hear, O heavens," was not merely an accusation; it was prophecy.
Heaven would one day *hear* again, when the blood of His Son spoke better things than that of Abel.

5. Chronology — The Echo Through Ages

From Adam's fall to this final generation, the same verdict resounds. Every age begins in revelation and declines in rebellion. But every decline provokes a new dawn. Now the time of the end approaches; the same cry goes forth again:

> *"Hear, O heavens, give ear, O earth."*

The Father is summoning His true Israel, the spiritual remnant, to arise in remembrance and repentance before the trumpet of judgment sounds.

6. Typology — The Pattern of the Prodigal

Israel's rebellion mirrors the parable of the prodigal son.
Fed, blessed, and adorned, he left the Father's house seeking freedom without fellowship. But famine found him.
It was hunger, not punishment, that brought him home.
Likewise, the Father allows shaking not to destroy, but to awaken.
He calls not for slaves, but for sons who remember; sons who will return not with gifts, but with tears.

7. Technology — The Prophetic Call in the Modern World

In this digital age, noise has replaced knowledge. Many hear, but few *listen.* The heavens still speak through every medium through Word, vision, and sound, calling a generation addicted to distraction back to stillness. The "network" of heaven is alive: prophetic voices rising across continents, declaring,

> *"Return to your first love. Return to the altar. Return to the Spirit."*

Technology itself becomes a vessel of witness, either amplifying rebellion or carrying the cry of repentance.

The Call to Return

This chapter is not history; it is a mirror. Every rebellion, every cold altar, every divided heart echoes the Father's sorrow.
Yet grace still speaks:

> *"Come now, and let us reason together, saith the Lord: though your sins be as scarlet, they shall be as white as snow."*

The heavens are listening.
The earth bears witness.
And the Father waits not for a perfect people,
but for a repentant one, who will hear His voice once more and say,
"Abba, we remember."

CHAPTER 2

The Great Day of the LORD
(Zephaniah 1:1–18 KJV)

"Hold thy peace at the presence of the Lord GOD: for the day of the LORD is at hand…"

Heaven's silence thickens; not as absence, but as anticipation. Creation holds its breath. The trumpets have not yet sounded, but their echoes tremble within the Spirit. For the day of the LORD is near; nearer than it has ever been; the day when mercy and judgment meet face to face, and the King steps forth from His dwelling to reckon with the nations and to refine His Bride. The Spirit of prophecy declares: *"Hold thy peace."* Cease from vain noise, from arguments and appearances. Stand still, for the Lord is arising from His holy habitation. He is weighing the hearts of men, not by words, but by fire.

1. Spiritology — The Fire that Searches the Spirit

The day of the LORD begins not in the clouds, but in the spirit realm. Before it manifests in the natural, it unfolds as divine inspection in the invisible. The Lord says, *"I will search Jerusalem with candles.*" The candle is the spirit of man (***Proverbs 20:27***), and the Lord Himself lights that candle to expose the hidden chambers within. Every unrepented motive, every secret allegiance, every idol of self will be revealed. This is not wrath without reason; it is purification before manifestation. The Spirit's fire searches not to condemn, but to cleanse; not to destroy, but to distinguish.

In this hour, the Spirit of the Lord moves through the Church, sifting wheat from chaff, vessels of light from vessels of shadow. The careless who once said, "The LORD will not do good, neither will He do evil," shall find that neutrality is rebellion, and silence is agreement with darkness.

2. Soulogy — The Weighing of Desire

The soul is the battlefield of the Day of the LORD. Here, judgment feels like inner turmoil, for the fire of conviction meets the resistance of the will. Zephaniah's words pierce the heart of every generation that lives self-satisfied, where comfort has replaced consecration, and entertainment has silenced intercession.

The Lord now searches the emotions and ambitions of His people.
What is loved more than His presence?
What is desired more than His will?
For wherever desire outgrows devotion, there an idol is born. Thus, the day of the LORD reveals the idolatries of the heart; not to humiliate, but to heal through holy fear.

3. Physiology — Signs in the Earth and the Body

When the heavens shift, the earth responds. The Day of the LORD shakes not only nations but nature. Winds, earthquakes, pestilences, and fires are not random events; they are the groans of a creation awaiting redemption. The blood of the innocent cries from the ground; the seas roar against corruption; and the very climate bears witness to moral decay.

Even the human body reflects divine shaking: sicknesses that arise from disobedience, weariness birthed from spiritual neglect, and strength renewed in those who dwell in the secret place. As in Zephaniah's vision, the judgment touches every layer of life: the land, the city, and the flesh that forgets its Maker.

4. Theology — The Day of Divine Reckoning

The "day of the LORD" is not one single date, but the unfolding of divine justice across time and eternity. It is the hour when every false balance is corrected, and the Kingdom of Heaven asserts its supremacy over human empires.

Zephaniah saw it: men building fortunes upon oppression, priests defiling truth with compromise, leaders mocking prophecy as ancient myth. But God's patience is not weakness; His silence is not forgetfulness. He will rise in the appointed hour to judge every system that denies His sovereignty. Yet, even in wrath, He remembers mercy; for those who cry out in repentance shall find refuge in the shadow of His wings.

5. Chronology — The Nearness of the Hour

Prophetic time is accelerating. Zephaniah's words have come full circle; the conditions of his generation mirror ours: lawlessness, deception, pride, and indifference. The Spirit whispers: *"The day of the LORD hastens greatly."* This is not the hour for slumber or speculation, but for alignment. The lamp must be filled, the garments washed, the altar restored.

We stand at the junction of mercy and judgment; two rivers converging into one flood of divine fulfilment.
Soon, silence will break into thunder.

6. Typology — The Searchlight in Jerusalem

"Jerusalem" in prophecy speaks of the Church; the place of His name. Thus, when God says, *"I will search Jerusalem with candles,"* He means He will search His house.

Every congregation, every pulpit, every heart becomes a chamber under divine inspection. The careless saints, content with form without fire, will be startled by the light of His presence. But those who have kept their lamps burning will shine brighter in the darkness, for judgment always begins where glory is meant to dwell.

As in Egypt, when the destroyer passed through the land, only the houses marked by blood were spared. So shall it be again: those sealed by the Spirit, covered in the Lamb, shall stand unmoved while the earth trembles under the weight of His appearing.

7. Technology — The Trumpet in the Digital Age

The modern world amplifies prophecy at the speed of light. The Word travels through networks, satellites, and screens, but so does deception. The same airwaves that carry truth also carry lies. Thus, the Spirit warns: *"Be careful what you hear."* Discernment is the firewall of the saints.

The digital candle is burning in this generation; messages, dreams, and revelations sent across continents like lightning. This too is the searching of Jerusalem: every screen a mirror, every word a test. Will technology serve the trumpet of truth or the whisper of Babylon? The answer will reveal the heart.

The Final Cry

The day of the LORD is not terror for the righteous, but triumph for the faithful.
To the world, it is darkness; to the Bride, it is dawn.
For the King comes to cleanse, not merely to punish.
He comes to reclaim what is His: hearts, nations, altars, and crowns.

Therefore, *"Hold thy peace at the presence of the Lord GOD."*
Be still, not in fear, but in awe.
The shaking is His movement.
The thunder is His mercy in disguise.
And when He speaks again, the heavens will open, the earth will bow, and the cry shall rise from Zion
"The Lord, He is God!"

CHAPTER 3

Gather Yourselves, O Nation Not
Desired
(Zephaniah 2:1–4 KJV)

"Before the decree bring forth... seek ye the LORD, all ye meek of the earth..."

Message (The Call of the Spirit):

Before the storm breaks, heaven opens a final window; mercy is extended before judgment descends. The Spirit moves through the earth whispering, "Gather yourselves." It is not a political gathering, nor a denominational one; it is the convergence of the broken, the meek, the undefiled in heart. This call is not geographical; it is spiritual. It resounds within souls who still tremble at the Word, those who know the voice of the Shepherd amid the roar of confusion. The decree has not yet been brought forth, but the clouds are heavy with prophecy. Time bends toward its appointed hour. Grace waits only for obedience.

Mystery (The Spiritology of Gathering):
In the courts of heaven, decrees are living scrolls; words sealed until faith awakens them. To "gather" is to come into alignment with the Spirit's government; to stand under the banner of holiness, clothed with the garments of the meek. Zion is not a mountain of dust; it is a people of rest, a habitation of the Spirit prepared through repentance.

The meek carry heaven's weight because they are emptied of self. In them, the fire does not consume; it refines. They are the vessels by which God will preserve the earth from total ruin.

Mandate (The Application in the Earth):
Every believer must return to the altar within. Every household must restore Sabbath order[the pattern of rest, purity, and communion. Every nation must choose: Will it be ruled by the spirit of Babel or governed by the Spirit of Truth?

Now is the hour of separation. The proud will scatter; the meek will inherit. The decree soon brings forth, and only those hidden in obedience will stand when the wind of the LORD blows through the land.

7-Dimensional Flow of the Word — "Gather Yourselves, O Nation Not Desired"

- **Spiritology:** Gathering by the breath of the Spirit, not by institution.

- **Soulogy:** The will submits, the emotions bow, the mind awakens.

- **Physiology:** The body becomes a living altar — separated from pollution.

- **Theology:** Divine justice and mercy kiss in the covenant of peace.

- **Chronology:** The final pause before the decree seals time.

- **Typology:** Noah's ark before the flood, Zion before the shaking.

- **Technology:** The Word transmitted as sound — the trumpet cry through prophetic vessels.

1. Spiritology — The Breath that Calls the Remnant

The gathering is not commanded by man's voice, but by the wind of the Spirit moving upon the deep once more. He calls from within, not from without, summoning those whose spirits are alive to His frequency. Each son and daughter hears a sound not of this world; the same breath that raised Adam now quickens Zion. The Spirit is forming one Body out of many fragments, knitting the scattered members into a living tabernacle of light. It is a reunion of breath with purpose, of Spirit with spirit; the true Israel awakened from sleep.

2. Soulogy — The Alignment of the Inner Realms

The gathering begins when the soul bows to the Spirit. The will ceases striving and yields; the emotions are sanctified and no longer ruled by fear; the intellect surrenders its pride and drinks from wisdom's well. The carnal mind, once divided, now becomes a mirror, reflecting the mind of Christ. In this humility, the soul finds its true rest; no longer torn between worlds, but fixed upon the eternal, anchored in peace.

3. Physiology — The Altar of the Body

The body becomes the visible sanctuary of invisible obedience. The flesh, once ruled by appetite, now submits to Spirit governance. Hands that once grasped now give; lips that once complained now bless; eyes once clouded now see light. The Lord walks again in His temple, not in stone, but in the sanctified frame of redeemed men and women. This is holiness embodied; the Sabbath restored in flesh.

4. Theology — The Covenant of Justice and Mercy

Here, heaven and earth embrace. Justice, long delayed, now meets mercy in the covenant of peace. The cross stands as the eternal equation: judgment absorbed, mercy released.
The Father's wrath and compassion converge in the pierced heart of the Son.
Every decree finds its fulfilment in Him: the Alpha of promise and the Omega of recompense. Those who gather under His name are gathered under His blood,
and through that blood, heaven's government finds its rest.

5. Chronology — The Moment Before the Seal

There is a silence in the heavens; not of absence, but of holy suspense. Prophetic time has entered its narrowing funnel. The decree hovers, the angels stand in readiness, the trumpets await command. This is the pause before fulfilment: the calm before the final act of mercy closes. Every clock on earth ticks toward convergence. The wise discern the hour; the foolish debate the season. Soon, time will yield to eternity.

6. Typology — The Pattern Before the Shaking

As it was in the days of Noah, so it is again. The ark is not made of wood this time; it is fashioned in Spirit and sealed by truth. The call is not to flee to mountains, but to ascend in the Spirit. Zion is the ark; the meek are its inhabitants. As judgment waters rise, those who are hidden in covenant will float upon peace. The shaking will expose foundations; every false tower will crumble, but the hill of the Lord will stand forever.

7. Technology — The Trumpet of the Word

Heaven transmits through sound, and the Spirit translates through vessels. The prophets are frequencies, the apostles conduits, the remnant amplifiers. The Word is no longer bound to scrolls or pulpits; it rides upon waves of light and breath. Each voice that speaks truth becomes a trumpet, announcing the King's approach. What was once confined to the upper room now fills the airwaves of creation. This is divine communication; Spirit-to-spirit technology, the convergence of Word, Wind, and Witness before the end unfolds.

CHAPTER 4

The End Is Come Upon the Four Corners
(Ezekiel 7:1–10 KJV)

"An end, the end is come upon the four corners of the land..."

MESSAGE — The Decree of Final Reckoning

The Word of the Lord now moves across the earth like lightning crossing the horizon. No nation, no throne, no institution is beyond its reach. The four winds stand at the edges of creation: north, south, east, and west, awaiting the voice that will release the final convergence.

The end is not destruction alone; it is divine completion. The scroll of time is folding upon itself, and the Spirit is gathering every unfinished word into the Book of Fulfilment.

The LORD will recompense every man according to his works. He is not mocked: He is exact.

The balances of heaven are being weighed with holy fire, and all flesh shall know that He alone is LORD.

The hour of silence has passed; the trumpet of exposure sounds. Hidden motives are being judged, secret covenants uncovered, and every false foundation, whether political, religious, or personal, is being shaken to reveal what cannot be moved.

The markets of sin collapse, the altars of self crumble, and the alliances of darkness fall into confusion. The Lord's fury is not chaos; it is perfect justice dressed in glory. He is measuring time by righteousness, not by calendars.

MYSTERY — The Four Corners and the Eternal Cross

In spiritology, the "four corners" mark the full compass of creation; the design of the divine cross stretched across heaven and earth.
North — the place of judgment.
South — the realm of mercy.
East — the dawn of glory.
West — the setting of grace.
When all four converge, the cycle of redemption closes.

This is the architecture of divine finality:
the Lamb slain from the foundation now reigns from the fourfold throne.
What began in Eden ends in Zion. The garden has become a city; the city a Bride.
And the Spirit says: "Behold, I make all things new."

In soulogy, the four corners mirror the full man: mind, will, emotion, and conscience. Each realm must be purified lest corruption spread from within. The end begins internally before it manifests externally. When the soul is cleansed, the man is sealed; when rebellion persists, the man collapses under his own idols.

In theology, this "end" is the beginning of eternal reign; the

transition from grace to glory,
from invitation to separation.

MANDATE — The Call to Stand in the Final Hour

Now the Lord commands His remnant: "Stand at your post. Let your garments be white and your lamps burning." Do not join the panic of the nations, for fear is the false prophet of the end.

Build your altars in righteousness. Seal your homes in prayer and covenant. Let your worship rise as incense before the throne. The shaking is not your destruction; it is your distinction.

Zion must not fear the end; Zion *is* the end: the conclusion of God's plan, the embodiment of His rest.
As the systems fall, the sons rise.
As the world cries "collapse," heaven proclaims "completion."
The end is not the ruin of the righteous but the unveiling of the Bride.

7-DIMENSIONAL FLOW OF THE WORD — The End in Divine Fullness

2. Spiritology — The Winds of Judgment and Renewal

The Spirit rides upon the four winds, releasing both cleansing and correction. One wind uproots, another refines, another gathers, and another seals. Each direction carries a divine function, and together they form the breath of restoration across the nations. The end is not the ceasing of breath but the sanctification of it; the world inhaling the final move of the Holy Spirit before the King appears.

2. Soulogy — The Unveiling of Hidden Motives

The soul stands naked before divine inspection. Thoughts are weighed, intentions revealed. No mask endures before the fire of truth. Every emotion must bow to the Spirit; every imagination must be brought captive. The end separates loyalty from lip service, revealing those who serve God for love, not gain.

3. Physiology — The Earth and the Body Shaking Together

The dust groans with creation's travail. Earthquakes mirror inner quakes; both are longing for liberation. Man's body, formed from soil, trembles as the ground trembles. Yet the righteous shall not be moved, for their temple is founded on the Rock. The final fire will refine the flesh into obedience; the mortal yielding to the immortal, the corruptible swallowed by glory.

4. Theology — The Justice of the Throne Manifested

Every doctrine now meets its verdict. What was preached in part is now judged in whole. The Lamb and the Lion sit upon one throne; the mercy that once pleaded now reigns with authority. The law and the prophets converge in Christ, and the covenant stands as the final constitution of eternity.

5. Chronology — The Collapse of Measured Time

The prophetic clock now strikes alignment. The seventh seal trembles; the trumpet's breath gathers. Time itself is folding; seasons overlap, generations converge, and what took centuries to unfold now manifests in moments. Eternity presses against the edges of history, and those attuned to the Spirit already hear the footsteps of the King.

6. Typology — The Echoes of Prophetic Patterns

Noah built; Lot fled; Daniel stood; John beheld. Every shadow now merges into the substance; the ark becomes the Bride, the wilderness becomes the Kingdom, and the throne descends to dwell among men. This is the full circle of redemption: the Alpha calling forth His Omega.

7. Technology — The Trumpet Transmission of the End-Time Word

Heaven's frequencies now fill the air; satellites, streams, and voices become vessels of divine utterance. The Spirit harnesses the language of light and sound, declaring through every medium: *"The end is come."* This is not doom; it is delivery. The trumpet of truth is sounding through prophetic networks, and those with ears to hear are being sealed by revelation.

CHAPTER 5

The Trumpet to All Nations
(Isaiah 18:3 KJV)

"All ye inhabitants of the world, and dwellers on the earth, see ye, when he lifteth up an ensign on the mountains; and when he bloweth a trumpet, hear ye."

MESSAGE — The Banner of the Returning King

T he trumpet is no longer distant. Its vibration moves through the atmosphere of every continent; not the brass of men, but the breath of God sounding through His chosen.

The ensign is lifted; the standard of the Lamb and the Lion. It waves not in fabric but in fire; not on a pole, but upon the hearts of His witnesses. From the mountains of revelation, Zion above all peaks; the banner gleams with eternal light. It is the signal to gather, the mark of separation between kingdom and chaos.

Nations hear, yet few discern. Kings assemble in counsel, but heaven speaks beyond their microphones. Africa stirs in prophetic remembrance; the cradle and crown of covenant memory. Israel awakens; the seed and the sign. The islands of the sea echo with the cry, "Prepare ye the way of the Lord."

This is the hour of global witness. Every tribe, tongue, and nation stands within the circle of His call. The gospel of the Kingdom, not the religion of men, shall sound to the ends of the earth. And when the last trumpet of truth resounds, the heavens will open, and the Son of Man shall be seen upon the clouds, robed in light, crowned with judgment, bearing the wounds that purchased the world.

Zion rises; not as geography but as habitation, not as religion but as revelation, not as a mountain of dust but as a dwelling of Spirit. She is the voice of the Bride and the fire of the altar; the city that cannot be hidden.

MYSTERY — The Ensign of Heaven's Government

In Spiritology, the *ensign* is the banner of divine order; the visible sign of invisible government. When it is lifted, authority transfers; old dominions fall, new realms awaken.

In soulology, it is the call of identity; each nation must remember its divine name, each people their prophetic root. The tribes of the earth are not random; they are echoes of an eternal pattern. The Spirit calls them back to their true inheritance, not of land, but of light.

In physiology, the ensign is lifted upon the body of Christ, a living mountain, formed of many members. His blood is the scarlet thread; His Spirit the wind that waves it.
Through His Body, the signal of heaven is made flesh again in earth.

Theologically, the ensign is the unveiling of Christ's dominion; the government of God returning to rule through mercy and justice. It is Isaiah's prophecy fulfilled: "The government shall be upon His shoulder."

Chronologically, it is the trumpet before the end; the global witness spoken by Jesus in **Matthew 24:14**. Before the end, there must be testimony; before the closing, a proclamation. This trumpet is sounding now.

Typologically, the ensign recalls Moses' staff lifted in the wilderness, the serpent raised, the standard of healing and victory. Now, the Son of Man is lifted once more, and all who look shall live.

Technologically, the signal travels by wind and wavelength; prophetic frequencies riding digital streams and earthly signals. The gospel runs through fibre and cloud, for creation itself has become a conduit of divine broadcast. Heaven's trumpet now sounds through every channel; the Spirit translating the Word in every tongue.

MANDATE — The Call to Rise as the Banner

The time for silence is over. Every believer is summoned to become a signal, a living banner of light. This trumpet is not for the clergy alone; it is for witnesses. The Spirit says, *"Lift up your voice like a trumpet."*

Let Africa bear the sound of awakening;
let Israel declare the covenant fulfilled;
let the islands send the echo across the seas.

You are the mountain upon which the banner is raised. Let holiness be your height, truth your pole, love your flag. Lift Christ high until every knee bows, every tongue confesses,
and every nation beholds His glory.

The trumpet calls not to fear, but to faith. Not to despair, but to dominion. For as the world trembles, Zion sings. The Kingdom of God is not in retreat; it is in revelation.

7-DIMENSIONAL FLOW OF THE WORD — The Ensign of All Ages

1. Spiritology — The Breath of the Trumpet

The trumpet is the breath of the Spirit passing through surrendered vessels. Every true voice is wind meeting word; sound born of surrender. This is the communication of heaven through human lungs. When the Spirit blows, the voice becomes flame, and the message travels beyond borders, beyond language, beyond time.

2. Soulogy — The Awakening of Nations

The trumpet pierces the inner ear of nations. Identity buried in centuries of deception now begins to stir. The sons of Africa rise to remember their priestly root; the scattered tribes hear the call of the covenant once more. The collective soul of humanity is being summoned to repentance and restoration.

3. Physiology — The Banner Made Flesh

The body of Christ becomes the mountain of God; living stones stacked in alignment, shining with His glory. Every believer is a fibre in the fabric of His flag. The raising of hands in worship becomes the lifting of the ensign. Through consecrated bodies, the invisible kingdom takes form upon the visible earth.

4. Theology — The Government of the Lamb

Upon His shoulder rests the administration of eternity. Every dominion of men must now submit to His throne. The cross remains the centre of power; the flagpole of divine reign. Through His resurrection, the banner was raised forever; a signal that death is defeated and the King is alive.

5. Chronology — The Trumpet Before the Dawn

Prophetic time now leans into acceleration. The trumpet of witness sounds before the trumpet of war. Before Christ returns in glory, He returns in the gospel, riding the wings of His Word across nations. Every person must hear, for love demands no soul be left untouched.

6. Typology — The Banner of Redemption

As Moses lifted the serpent, as David raised the standard, as Isaiah saw the root of Jesse stand for an ensign of the people; so now the risen Christ is lifted upon the mountain of the Spirit. Those who look to Him are healed; those who hide from Him are judged. The pattern repeats, fulfilled in fire and glory.

7. Technology — The Voice That Fills the Earth

Heaven's trumpet now speaks through digital tongues; prophecy through broadcast, intercession through network, light through data. What once was spoken in tents is now transmitted through time. This is divine technology; Spirit flowing through sound, word, and image to reach every ear before the end.

The trumpet of the Lord is the final transmission of truth, and those who hear will rise.

CHAPTER 6

The Sign of the Temple
(Matthew 24:2 KJV)

"See ye not all these things? verily I say unto you, There shall not be left here one stone upon another, that shall not be thrown down."

The Master's words still roll through the corridors of time, breaking the silence of the proud, unseating the thrones of flesh. What man has called "holy" but God has not built, shall not endure. Every counterfeit altar trembles; every monument raised by vanity begins to crack beneath the gaze of the Eternal Builder.

This is not chaos; it is calibration. The Spirit is aligning the earth to the blueprint of Heaven. He is dismantling the architecture of pride, tearing down the cathedrals of control, the economies of deception, and the governments of rebellion. Every stone laid by ambition is being overturned, that the Cornerstone might again be seen and honoured.

The shaking is not for destruction but for distinction. Gold must be separated from clay; glory from glitter. The temple He seeks cannot be touched by human hands; it breathes, it lives, it burns. The Holy Ghost is gathering His stones from every nation:
— From Africa, the cry of restoration.
— From Israel, the memory of the covenant.

— From the islands, the echo of prophecy.
Each one washed in the blood, fitted by revelation, sealed by the fire of His Spirit.

Behold, the mystery of the true Temple:
It is not in Jerusalem's dust nor Rome's marble, but in the yielded hearts of the redeemed. The walls are made of witnesses, the foundation of apostles, the gates of praise. The High Priest walks not in robes but in glory, and the altar burns not with beasts but with surrendered souls.

Every shaking we see in nations, in churches, in the deep places of the soul, is the voice of Christ still saying, *"See ye not all these things?"* For He is returning not to a building but to a Body. Not to an institution, but to an indwelling. The temple of flesh must fall that the temple of Spirit may rise.

This is the sign of the end and the beginning:
The fall of human systems, and the rise of the eternal temple of the Holy Ghost. The kingdom that cannot be moved is already forming within. And from its unseen stones, Zion is being revealed; a city not built by man, but by God Himself.

CHAPTER 7

Even So, Come, Lord Jesus
(Revelation 22:20 KJV)

"He which testifieth these things saith, Surely I come quickly. Amen.
Even so, come, Lord Jesus."

he Spirit whispers what creation shouts:
He is coming. Not in secret shadow, not as a tale told by trembling lips; but in the full brightness of unveiled glory. Heaven leans closer, time holds its breath, and the pulse of prophecy quickens.

The Bride groans.
Her longing has matured into travail; she no longer prays for things, but for Him. Every sigh, every tear, every righteous cry beneath oppression becomes incense before His throne. The Spirit joins her voice; the deep calling unto Deep; until both heaven and earth harmonise in one cry:

"Come."

The earth groans.
The soil remembers Eden; the seas remember the Word that tamed them. Volcanoes, storms, and quakes are not chaos; they are contractions, labouring toward new creation. Even the stars dim in anticipation, for the Light that made them draws near again. Every system built on decay is unravelling; every false dominion is gasping its last breath. The old world is passing, and the Kingdom that cannot be shaken is pressing through the veil.

And the Spirit groans.
He searches the hearts of men, refining the remnant, sealing the faithful. His fire burns away the mixture, His wind gathers the elect, His waters cleanse the Bride's garments until she shines like morning. He is preparing a habitation worthy of the King's descent, not of stone, but of surrendered souls.

"Surely I come quickly."

These are not words of delay but of divine imminence. Every heartbeat draws history nearer to its holy conclusion. The trumpet is already in the mouth of the archangel; the scroll of nations is nearly complete. The Lamb who once came in weakness shall return in fire; eyes burning, voice roaring, feet upon the mountains of Zion.

And the Bride answers with no hesitation:

"Even so, come, Lord Jesus."

For she knows that His coming is not to destroy her, but to dwell in her. Not to end her story, but to finish it in glory. The Spirit and the Bride are now one sound, one heartbeat, one flame.

The waiting is holy.
Every trial refines the wedding garment; every storm polishes the lamp of faith. For soon, very soon, the sky will split with light, and what was promised will stand before all eyes: The King of Glory, enthroned upon Zion, and the redeemed clothed in white, singing the ancient song made new —

"Behold, the tabernacle of God is with men."

BONUS

Author's Vision

BONUS 1

The Fire in the Midst of the City
(The River and the Throne —
Revelation 22:1–2 KJV)

"And he shewed me a pure river of water of life, clear as crystal, proceeding out of the throne of God and of the Lamb. In the midst of the street of it, and on either side of the river, was there the tree of life…"

The vision opens not with ruins, but with radiance. The city once judged is now transfigured; from its very heart burns a fire not of wrath, but of wonder.

Ezekiel saw it first, the glory departing from the temple and returning with a wheel of flame, a fire enfolded within itself.

John saw it fulfilled; the same glory now enthroned, the river of life flowing where once the altars bled.

This is *the fire in the midst of the city*: not consuming, but transforming. The Spirit of burning has finished His work; the dross is gone, and what remains is transparent as crystal.

The Lamb reigns from within: His throne no longer distant, but pulsing through every street, every heart, every stream of living light.

The river speaks.
Its sound is peace; yet its current carries judgment and mercy in perfect harmony.
It proceeds from the throne, not beside it, for every decree now flows as life, not law.
The same river that once flooded Eden's gates now restores what was lost.
Where sin carved deserts, grace plants gardens.
Where death reigned in silence, the trees clap their hands.

On either side of the river grows the Tree of Life — not one, but many, yet one in essence.
Each branch bears fruit for the nations,
each leaf a covenant of healing.
This is no metaphor — it is the revelation of the redeemed creation,
the earth baptized in glory, the heavens joined in worship.
The Lamb's light now illumines all; there is no temple, for the Lord God Almighty *is* the Temple.

And in the midst of it — the Fire.
It is the same holy flame that once dwelt between the cherubim,
that touched Isaiah's lips, that danced at Pentecost.
Now it fills the city entire.
Every soul becomes a living lamp,
every heart a throne where the King abides.
The fire that once judged now indwells;
the consuming becomes communion.

The nations walk in its brightness.
Kings bring their glory, not their pride.
Time itself dissolves into worship — the curse is gone,
and eternity breathes through every street of gold.
The Bride no longer waits; she reigns beside the Lamb,
her garments aflame with the same light that crowns Him.

This is the restoration foretold —
Eden reborn as Zion,
the altar reborn as a river,
the fire reborn as love.

And from the throne, still, the voice speaks:

"Behold, I make all things new."

BONUS 2

The Nations Bring Their Glory into
Zion
(Revelation 21:24–26 KJV)

"And the nations of them which are saved shall walk in the
light of it: and the kings of the earth do bring their glory
and honour into it.
And the gates of it shall not be shut at all by day: for there
shall be no night there.
And they shall bring the glory and honour of the nations
into it."

The vision widens now.

The city of fire becomes a city of nations; Zion radiant, breathing with eternal morning.

From the edges of the earth they come, tribes and tongues once scattered, now streaming upward like rivers returning to the source.

Every crown is laid down; every language becomes praise.

The Lamb reigns not from a throne apart, but from the centre of all life.

The gates — always open — breathe mercy, not defence.
No guard stands there, for nothing defiled can enter;
holiness itself is the boundary.
Here, glory travels freely,
not as conquest, but as offering.
Kings bring not wealth, but wisdom refined through trial —
their honour no longer political, but spiritual,
their thrones yielded to the One who reigns forever.

This is the divine reversal:
what Babylon stole, Zion restores;
what pride scattered, the Spirit gathers.
Every art, every culture, every sound redeemed —
folded into the great harmony of the Kingdom.
Gold returns to the streets;
music to the sanctuaries;
justice to the courts;
light to the eyes of every nation.

For this is not a city of one people only,
but the dwelling of all who overcame the beast by the blood of the
Lamb.
Its light is not borrowed; it *is* the Lamb.
Its song is not rehearsed; it *is* the breath of the redeemed.
And as they walk in the brightness of His presence,
time itself bows in silence — for day has no end.

The nations do not compete; they converge.
Each one carries its portion of divine revelation —
Ethiopia her endurance, Israel her covenant,
the Isles their worship, the East its wisdom,
the West its witness of grace.
All threads woven into one garment of light,
the robe of the Bride,
the covering of creation restored.

And the voice from the midst of the throne declares again:

"The tabernacle of God is with men."
Not as visitation, but habitation.
Not a holy place to visit, but a holy people to become.

The journey ends where it began; the Breath of God walking again among men, no veil, no temple, no distance.
The Sabbath fulfilled, the nations at rest, the glory returned to Zion.

BONUS 3

The Throne of the Lamb and His
Servants Shall Serve Him
(Revelation 22:3–5 KJV)

"And there shall be no more curse: but the throne of God
and of the Lamb shall be in it;
and his servants shall serve him:
And they shall see his face; and his name shall be in their
foreheads.
And there shall be no night there; and they need no candle,
neither light of the sun;
for the Lord God giveth them light: and they shall reign
for ever and ever."

The vision settles into stillness; holy stillness.
The trumpet has ceased, the thunder is quiet, and only light remains. From the throne at the centre of the city flows not decree, but communion. The curse has dissolved like mist before the dawn. The rebellion of Eden is fully undone; every scar of sin transfigured into song.
This is the consummation of the covenant:

"His servants shall serve Him." Not by obligation, but by union. Service here is worship, and worship is rulership; priests and kings bound in one flame of devotion. The hands that once toiled now heal; the voices that wept now govern. Authority is no longer hierarchy, but harmony. Each heart beats in rhythm with the King, and all creation moves to the pulse of His will.

The veil is gone.

No mediator stands between the soul and its Maker.

They shall *see His face.* What Moses could not behold, what angels veiled their wings to shield from, is now the inheritance of every redeemed one.

The light that once blinded now beautifies.

His name shines on their foreheads; identity restored, nature redefined, the mind sealed in the consciousness of divine sonship.

No night remains.

For the light that fills the city is not the radiance of the sun, but the revelation of the Son. No lamp burns, for the Lord Himself is illumination. The knowledge of the Lord fills every thought, every cell of creation alive with His awareness.

There is no end to the reign, for eternity is not a length of time, but the atmosphere of His presence.

And thus the prophecy returns full circle; from the fall to the fullness, from rebellion to rest.

The throne of God and the Lamb are one, Spirit and Word eternally enthroned in the midst of their people.

This is the true Sabbath: not a day, but a dwelling; not cessation, but consummation; the rest of God finally found in man.

The reign of the Lamb is the reign of love.

It governs not by fear, but by fire; a fire that refines, that renews, that reignites creation's original harmony.

The redeemed serve not because they must, but because His glory has become their nature.

They reign not by command, but by communion, their crowns woven from worship, their thrones built of light.

And the Spirit concludes what began in Genesis:
God and man together again,
the Word made flesh,
the flesh made Word.
The eternal temple breathes.
The city shines.
The Sabbath lives.

"And they shall reign for ever and ever."

PRECEPT GIVEN BY THE LORD JESUS

3-Modes × 7-Dimensions

ISAIAH 1:2-4

2 Hear, O heavens, and give ear, O earth: for the Lord hath spoken, I have nourished and brought up children, and they have rebelled against me.

3 The ox knoweth his owner, and the ass his master's crib: but Israel doth not know, my people doth not consider.

4 Ah sinful nation, a people laden with iniquity, a seed of evildoers, children that are corrupters: they have forsaken the Lord, they have provoked the Holy One of Israel unto anger, they are gone away backward.

And we interpret this with the mind of our generation, the urgency of His soon return, and the full **Teaching Protocol + 3 Modes × 7 Dimensions (3M7D)** fused into one prophetic transmission.

MODE 1 — Vision

The heavens are summoned as witnesses. This is not poetry; it is legal language in the divine courtroom.
The Father's voice echoes through creation; His grief becomes decree.

The heavens record rebellion, the earth bears its fruit.
In the Spirit, the Lord shows Isaiah the courtroom of eternity where the Father testifies against His own children.
The grief of God is not weakness; it is love dishonoured.

MODE 2 — Written

Isaiah inscribes a covenant charge. His pen becomes a trumpet.
Every word is both history and prophecy; Israel's story and our generation's mirror.
God's children have forgotten their Source.
They feed on doctrine yet hunger for presence.
They call Him Lord but resist His nature.
The ink of the prophet is witness; it marks the record for judgment and mercy alike.

MODE 3 — Spoken

Now the Word speaks again.
The Spirit cries through this generation: *"Hear, O heavens — give ear, O earth!"*
The Lord's tone has not softened.
His call is revival born from repentance.
He says to His Church: "I raised you in truth, but you have built altars to ambition.
Return to Me. I am not a memory — I am your Maker."

THE 7-DIMENSIONAL FLOW (3M7D)

1. **Spiritology:** The Father's Spirit is revealed as both Judge and Lover — the Breath that once gave life now groans in sorrow. The rebellion of sons quenches His wind; the restoration will begin when hearts exhale pride and inhale His Spirit again.

2. **Soulogy:** The mind forgets, the emotions wander, the will rebels. Sin begins in amnesia — the soul forgetting who raised it. The cure is remembrance — worship that restores identity.

3. **Physiology:** The body of believers mirrors Israel's decay: altars without fire, temples without glory. The Lord calls for consecration of flesh — holiness in action, not in name.

4. **Theology:** God's justice is relational, not mechanical. He disciplines as a Father, not as an executioner. His grief is divine pedagogy — correction leading back to communion.

5. **Chronology:** The rebellion of ancient Israel repeats in the digital age. The same pattern — abundance birthing arrogance — is unfolding before the end. History is prophecy on replay.

6. **Typology:** The ox and the ass — humble beasts — become symbols of those who still recognize their Master. The irony is divine: creation remembers what man forgets.

7. **Technology:** Today, the same cry rides through frequencies and fiber optics — "Hear, O heavens." Every signal, broadcast, and digital word becomes a vessel of the Voice. The Spirit now uses the airwaves once polluted by rebellion to call back the sons of God.

Prophetic Summation:
The Father's cry still shakes the heavens.
His grief is not against the world, but for His house.
He calls His children home before the final shaking.

"Return unto Me, for I am thy rest."

ZEPHANIAH 1:1–18

Theme: *The Searchlight of the Spirit and the Collapse of Idols*

1 The word of the Lord which came unto Zephaniah the son of Cushi, the son of Gedaliah, the son of Amariah, the son of Hizkiah, in the days of Josiah the son of Amon, king of Judah.

2 I will utterly consume all things from off the land, saith the LORD.

3 I will consume man and beast; I will consume the fowls of the heaven, and the fishes of the sea, and the stumbling blocks with the wicked: and I will cut off man from off the land, saith the LORD.

4 I will also stretch out mine hand upon Judah, and upon all the inhabitants of Jerusalem; and I will cut off the remnant of Baal from this place, and the name of the Chemarims with the priests;

5 And them that worship the host of heaven upon the

housetops; and them that worship and that swear by the LORD, and that swear by Malcham;

6 And them that are turned back from the LORD; and those that have not sought the LORD, nor enquired for him.

7 Hold thy peace at the presence of the LORD God: for the day of the Lord is at hand: for the LORD hath prepared a sacrifice, he hath bid his guests.

8 And it shall come to pass in the day of the LORD's sacrifice, that I will punish the princes, and the king's children, and all such as are clothed with strange apparel.

9 In the same day also will I punish all those that leap on the threshold, which fill their masters' houses with violence and deceit.

10 And it shall come to pass in that day, saith the LORD, that there shall be the noise of a cry from the fish gate, and an howling from the second, and a great crashing from the hills.

11 Howl, ye inhabitants of Maktesh, for all the merchant people are cut down; all they that bear silver are cut off.

12 And it shall come to pass at that time, that I will search Jerusalem with candles, and punish the men that are settled on their lees: that say in their heart, The LORD will not do good, neither will he do evil.

13 Therefore their goods shall become a booty, and their houses a desolation: they shall also build houses, but not inhabit them; and they shall plant vineyards, but not drink the wine thereof.

14 The great day of the LORD is near, it is near, and hasteth greatly, even the voice of the day of the LORD: the mighty man shall cry there bitterly.

15 That day is a day of wrath, a day of trouble and distress, a day of wasteness and desolation, a day of darkness and gloominess, a day of clouds and thick darkness,

16 A day of the trumpet and alarm against the fenced cities, and against the high towers.

17 And I will bring distress upon men, that they shall walk like blind men, because they have sinned against the LORD: and their blood shall be poured out as dust, and their flesh as the dung.

18 Neither their silver nor their gold shall be able to deliver them in the day of the LORD's wrath; but the whole land shall be devoured by the fire of his jealousy: for he shall make even a speedy riddance of all them that dwell in the land.

This is one of the most severe prophetic chapters in Scripture, and one of the most necessary for our generation.
It is a blueprint of the **end**, the **shaking**, and the **final awakening**.

MODE 1 — VISION

The prophet sees a world standing on a divine threshold.
He hears the silence before the storm; the stillness that belongs only to God.
The Spirit walks through Jerusalem with a candle, which is not a flame but a **searchlight**.
It passes through every room, every motive, every altar.

This is the Lord inspecting His people before judgment touches the nations.

The markets of vanity glow like embers in the dark.
The towers of pride tremble.
The idols of silver and gold whisper in fear, for they know they cannot ransom a soul.

And then Zephaniah sees it; **the Day of the LORD is approaching like a wave of fire wrapped in justice and truth.**

It is not chaos.
It is order returning.
A world out of alignment meeting the God of alignment.

MODE 2 — WRITTEN

Zephaniah records the decree as a legal proclamation:

The Lord will sweep. The Lord will search. The Lord will silence.

Every verse becomes a strike of the gavel.
The written word unveils the spiritual mechanics of judgment:

- Reversal of pride

- Exposure of corruption

- Collapse of false worship

- End of complacency

- Separation of holy from unholy

- Purging of mixture

- The rise of the remnant

The pages burn with the seriousness of God.
This is the chapter Jesus quietly referenced when He warned, "Watch."
The written word becomes a document of accountability for the last generation.

MODE 3 — SPOKEN

Now the Spirit speaks again not through Zephaniah only, but through every vessel aligned with His breath.

He says:

"Hold thy peace."
Stop your noise, your debates, your distractions.
My presence has entered the room.

"The day is near."
You cannot negotiate with time.
Heaven's clock is ahead of man's calendar.

"I will search with candles."
Not the world first — My house.
My people.
Their motives.
Their altars.
Their secret places.

"Neither silver nor gold shall deliver them."
Your currency cannot bribe eternity.
Your networks cannot negotiate your destiny.
Only repentance redeems.
Only obedience preserves.
Only purity shelters.

The Spoken Word becomes a trumpet; clear, sharp, unavoidable.

1. SPIRITOLOGY — The Searchlight of the Holy Spirit

The candle is the Spirit Himself. He does not search to condemn: He searches to expose what can no longer hide.
In the last days, conviction will intensify. The Spirit will walk the earth as a Refining Wind, separating true sons from cultural Christians.

His presence will reveal:
· hidden sins,
· lukewarm hearts,
· false worship,
· and unclean mixtures.

He searches not to shame but to save.

2. SOULOGY — The Collapse of Self-Reliance

This chapter dismantles the inner idols of man:
· pride that refuses correction,
· emotions untamed by holiness,
· minds numb to truth,

• wills resisting surrender.

The Day of the LORD is the day the soul loses the illusion of control.

3. PHYSIOLOGY — Bodies Out of Covenant

The people compromised physically:
• defiled altars,
• sensual worship,
• complacent lifestyles,
• bodies not yielded to God.

Judgment addresses what the body carries; actions, habits, practices.
The Lord restores holiness not as a doctrine but a discipline.

4. THEOLOGY — God as Judge and Father

Judgment is not divine rage, it is divine responsibility.
The Day of the LORD is the moment the Father removes everything that destroys His sons.
Justice is not revenge; it is the restoration of order.

5. CHRONOLOGY — The Acceleration of Prophetic Time

Zephaniah announces a time compression:
"The day is near — it is near."
What took generations will now take months.
Prophecy will stack, converge, and accelerate.
Time itself will obey the urgency of God.

6. TYPOLOGY — The Final Exodus

This chapter mirrors:
• Egypt before Passover,
• Babylon before Daniel's rise,
• Jerusalem before Christ's first coming.

The same patterns return before His second coming:
the purging of idols,

the dividing of hearts,
the rise of a remnant.

7. TECHNOLOGY — Judgment on Digital Idolatry

Today's idols are no longer carved — they are coded.
Screens become altars.
Feeds become teachers.
Platforms become gods.
But the Day of the LORD will sweep digital strongholds like ancient shrines.

The trumpet now blows through networks, satellites, and global communications.
The Word travels faster than rebellion.
The Spirit uses the same systems the enemy built, and redeploys them for truth.

Prophetic Summation of Precept 2

The Great Day of the LORD is not destruction for the remnant it is deliverance.

Everything built on pride will fall.
Everything established in truth will shine.
The Lord is not moving slowly
the Lord is moving surgically.

He searches to separate,
He judges to restore,
He shakes to awaken,
He warns to gather,
He calls to save.

And the cry remains:

Even so, Lord Jesus, come quickly.

ZEPHANIAH 2:1-4

Theme: *Forward-moving. Lyrical. Governance tone. Undiluted truth.*

1 Gather yourselves together, yea, gather together, O nation not desired;

2 Before the decree bring forth, before the day pass as the chaff, before the fierce anger of the Lord come upon you, before the day of the Lord's anger come upon you.

3 Seek ye the Lord, all ye meek of the earth, which have wrought his judgment; seek righteousness, seek meekness: it may be ye shall be hid in the day of the Lord's anger.

4 For Gaza shall be forsaken, and Ashkelon a desolation: they shall drive out Ashdod at the noon day, and Ekron shall be rooted up.

MODE 1 — VISION

What Zephaniah *saw* in the Spirit

1. Spiritology — The Gathering Wind of the Holy Spirit

The Spirit moves like a quiet but relentless stormfront.

He circles the earth, searching for a people who will gather *before* the decree is unleashed.

"Gather yourselves together, yea, gather together, O nation not desired."

This is not a suggestion; it is a summons from the Throne.

The Spirit separates wheat from chaff by summoning *before* He strikes.

2. Soulogy — The Call to Oneness Before Judgment

The fragmented soul of a scattered people hears the drumbeat of impending intervention.

Pride cracks.

Ego bends.

Identity is sifted.

A remnant realises:

"You cannot stand alone in the day of the LORD.

You must return to alignment before the decree births consequences."

3. Physiology — Bodies Moved Into Formation

Feet feel the urgency.

Hands sense the trembling.

Heartbeat aligns with prophetic timing.

The Spirit literally draws bodies together; into prayer, into obedience, into repentance, into divine strategy.

He forms a human infrastructure that can stand in the day of shaking.

4. Theology — The Gathering Before the Storm

Zephaniah reveals a corporate architecture of mercy:

God never judges without first offering a gathering.

Judgment is not a reaction.

Judgment is governance.

The "nation not desired" is called *before* the decree crystallises in heaven's court.

5. Chronology — The Window Before the Decree

There is a *before*.
There is an *after*.
Zephaniah stands in the doorway between the two.
The decree is already drafted.
Time is not waiting.
This is a pre-judgment corridor.
A short window, rapidly closing.

6. Typology — The Remnant Within the Refused Nation

Israel was a nation rejected by nations, dismissed by empires, and ignored by powers.
Yet God calls the undesired first, because the remnant is always hidden inside the rejected.
The nation the world does not desire is the nation God treasures.

7. Technology — The Divine System of Pre-Decree Alignment

Heaven runs on order.
Before a decree is executed, alignment is required.
The call to "gather" is the spiritual notification system.
It is the alert.
The early warning architecture.
If you respond, you enter immunity.
If you resist, you enter consequence.

MODE 2 — WRITTEN

What the Spirit carved into the text

1. Spiritology — Written Summons

The word "gather" appears twice because the Spirit is emphasizing urgency.
A double-call is never casual.

It is heavenly escalation.

2. Soulogy — Written Exposure

"Not desired" shows internal rejection, external rejection, and spiritual rejection; all three converging to create a people who must return home.

3. Physiology — Written Movement

"Before the decree bring forth" literally sketches an image of a pregnant judgment.
It has a due date.
It only waits for alignment.

4. Theology — Written Governance

The structure is procedural:
Gather → Seek → Hide → Survive.
God gives protocol before He gives verdict.

5. Chronology — Written Countdown

"Before the day pass as the chaff."
Time is pictured as dust blowing away; swift, fragile, irreversible.

6. Typology — Written Remnant Pattern

Every remnant in Scripture gathers *before* something breaks:
Noah before the flood.
Lot before the fire.
Moses before the angel passed through Egypt.
The remnant always moves first.

7. Technology — Written Warning System

The passage operates as a predictive model:
if gathering occurs → remnant preserved;
if gathering fails → judgment activates.

MODE 3 — SPOKEN

What the Spirit is saying *now*

1. Spiritology — "Return before I rise."

The Spirit speaks like thunder under the horizon:
"Gather. Now. Not tomorrow."

2. Soulogy — "Drop the divisions."

No personal empire will survive the day of the LORD.

3. Physiology — "Move your feet toward Zion."

Alignment requires literal motion.

4. Theology — "My decree is prepared."

Judgment is not emotional.
It is scheduled.

5. Chronology — "You are in the last stretch of 'before.'"

This is the final corridor of mercy.

6. Typology — "You are the remnant within the rejected."

The world may not desire you.
Heaven does.

7. Technology — "Activate gathering mode."

Build networks.
Call assemblies.
Finalise alignment.
Time is nearly exhausted.

Prophetic Summation of Precept 3

The window is open but narrowing.
The remnant must gather immediately.
Identity must align.
Structures must be formed.

The decree is drafted and poised for execution.
Those who heed the call enter preservation; those who delay are overtaken.

EZEKIEL 7:1-10

OVERVIEW — The Lord Speaks Into Our Generation

1 Moreover the word of the LORD came unto me, saying,

2 Also, thou son of man, thus saith the Lord God unto the land of Israel; An end, the end is come upon the four corners of the land.

3 Now is the end come upon thee, and I will send mine anger upon thee, and will judge thee according to thy ways, and will recompense upon thee all thine abominations.

4 And mine eye shall not spare thee, neither will I have pity: but I will recompense thy ways upon thee, and thine abominations shall be in the midst of thee: and ye shall know that I am the LORD.

5 Thus saith the Lord God; An evil, an only evil, behold, is come.

6 An end is come, the end is come: it watcheth for thee; behold, it is come.

7 The morning is come unto thee, O thou that dwellest in the land: the time is come, the day of trouble is near, and not the sounding again of the mountains.

8 Now will I shortly pour out my fury upon thee, and accomplish mine anger upon thee: and I will judge thee according to thy ways, and will recompense thee for all thine abominations.

9 And mine eye shall not spare, neither will I have pity: I will recompense thee according to thy ways and thine abominations that are in the midst of thee; and ye shall know that I am the Lord that smiteth.

10 Behold the day, behold, it is come: the morning is gone forth; the rod hath blossomed, pride hath budded.

Ezekiel 7 is not ancient thunder; it is *contemporary policy.* Jesus already signed the warning into the atmosphere:

"When you see these things… know that it is near, even at the doors."

Ezekiel 7 is the operational brief for the last days; the announcement that the old cycles have expired, the rebellion of nations is audited, and heaven's decree is moving from draft to execution.

Line 1–2 — "An End, the End, Is Come"

(The End of the Four Corners: Global, Total, Irreversible)

MODE 1 — VISION

1. Spiritology

The Spirit shows a horizon closing in like four walls tightening.
This is not regional judgment; it's *planetary convergence.*
North, south, east, west — all corners respond to one verdict.

2. Soulogy

Humanity feels the pressure of finality.
There's a low-grade dread running under the earth.
People sense something ending but cannot articulate it.

3. Physiology

Bodies react: unrest, agitation, confusion.
The end does not begin in politics; it begins in nervous systems.

4. Theology

God declares:
"Not an end — **the** end."
This is eschatological precision.
Cycles that tolerated delay are now closed.

5. Chronology

We have entered the terminal phase of the divine timetable.
The age is not winding down; it is *terminating.*

6. Typology

Four corners =
four winds,
four beasts,
four empires,
four dimensions of humanity.
All synchronized toward completion.

7. Technology

Heaven triggers an end-of-age protocol.
The system begins shutting down old patterns and activating kingdom architecture.

Line 3–4 — "My Eye Shall Not Spare"

(The Removal of Negotiation)

MODE 2 — WRITTEN

1. Spiritology

The Spirit shuts the mercy door assigned to rebellion.
This is not the shutting of grace; it is the shutting of *delay.*

2. Soulogy

Pride loses diplomatic immunity.
Hearts accustomed to loopholes discover that judgment is now architectural, not emotional.

3. Physiology

Bodies that refused repentance will feel the weight of consequences.
This is not punishment; it is consequence solidified.

4. Theology

"For thy abominations are in the midst of thee."
God judges from the inside out internals dictate externals.

5. Chronology

The time of pleading is replaced with the time of settling accounts.
Heaven moves from invitation to audit.

6. Typology

Every generation reaches a tipping point;
ours has reached it globally.
As in Noah's day, the decree shifts from *warning* to *performance.*

7. Technology

Heaven applies a mirrored-judgment system:
what you built returns to you,
what you sowed finds you,
what you empowered governs you.

Line 5–7 — "An Evil, an Only Evil… The Morning Is Come"

(The Dawn of Divine Interruption)

MODE 3 — SPOKEN (What the Spirit says now)

1. Spiritology — "Morning is coming, but not the morning you expect."

This is not sunrise for comfort this is sunrise for exposure.

2. Soulogy — "Your cycles of self-governance are expiring."

Nations can no longer outrun their own fruit.

3. Physiology — "Prepare your body for kingdom alignment."

The remnant must live alert, clean, ready, and mobile.

4. Theology — "My day interrupts your days."

God breaks into human calendars.
Heaven now leads the schedule.

5. Chronology — "The morning is here — the end of delay."

This verse announces prophetic dawn:
When morning comes, the window of hiding closes.

6. Typology — "As the morning exposed Adam, so shall it expose the world."

The glory-light reveals everything.

7. Technology — "The kingdom operating system is turning on."

New directives.
New alignments.
New judgments.
Nothing remains static.

Line 8–10 — "I Will Pour Out My Fury... Behold, It Is Come"

(The Activation of Final Justice)

Merged 3M7D Interpretation

1. Spiritology

Fury = the burning dimension of the Holy Spirit (*Isaiah 4:4*).
It is cleansing, not chaotic.

2. Soulogy

Human conscience will be forced to face itself.
Everything hidden becomes reportable.

3. Physiology

The earth shakes.
Structures fold.
What is corrupt collapses under its own weight.

4. Theology

"My fury will rest upon thee."

Judgment is not an explosion; it is a settling.

5. Chronology

This is the moment prophets across ages saw.
We are no longer reading prophecy
we are *standing inside it.*

6. Typology

Verse 10:
"Behold the day, behold it is come."
This is the same language Jesus used:
"It is near, even at the doors."

7. Technology

The divine decree is executed.
No further approvals.
No extensions.
The system moves into completion mode.

Prophetic Summation of Precept 4

Ezekiel 7 is the governance blueprint for the close of this age.
The decree is active.
The end is not future; it is operational.
The Spirit is calling the remnant into formation.
The world has crossed from warning to performance.
Christ's return is the next major event in the timetable of heaven.

ISAIAH 18:3

3 All ye inhabitants of the world, and dwellers on the earth, see ye, when he lifteth up an ensign on the mountains; and when he bloweth a trumpet, hear ye.

This is the global alert.
The universal memo.
The strategic broadcast from heaven's command centre.

Christ said He is coming quickly; Isaiah tells us how the world is signalled.

MODE 1 — VISION

(What the Spirit is showing)

1. Spiritology — The Ensign Is Not Cloth; It Is Christ.

In the Spirit, the banner raised over the mountains is *the Lamb enthroned.*
This is the appearance of His government above the chaos of nations.

2. Soulogy — Humanity Feels an Unnamed Pressure.

People sense the world is shifting.
Something is being "lifted up" beyond politics and conflict.

3. Physiology — Bodies Respond Before Minds Do.

Creation trembles.

Nations shake.

The sound reaches the body before the intellect.

4. Theology — God Is Summoning All Nations at Once.

This is not a word to Israel alone.

This is not selective prophecy.

It is **global summons**; inhabitants and dwellers without distinction.

5. Chronology — The Ensign Appears Before the Final Shaking.

Isaiah marks the sequence:

First the banner.

Then the trumpet.

Then the return of the King.

6. Typology — Moses Lifted the Serpent; Christ Lifts the Banner.

As the serpent was lifted for healing, so Christ is lifted for gathering; a prophetic inversion revealing the final harvest.

7. Technology — A Signal Protocol Activated in the Heavens.

Heaven issues a full-spectrum broadcast:

visual (ensign),

auditory (trumpet),

global (all inhabitants),

spiritual (mountain of God).

The system has gone live.

MODE 2 — WRITTEN

(What the Scripture establishes in structure)

1. Spiritology — Mountains = Realms of Authority.

The ensign is raised on the mountain of the Lord — unseen but unstoppable.

2. Soulogy — Nations Must "See."

This verse demands perception, not politics.
The Spirit is teaching the world how to interpret the times.

3. Physiology — The Trumpet Penetrates Human Atmosphere.

This is no earthly horn.
It confronts the flesh with heavenly sound.

4. Theology — God Commands Hearing and Seeing.

Two senses must awaken:
• spiritual sight
• spiritual hearing
This is the double witness of the last days.

5. Chronology — We Are in the Trumpet Window.

The ensign is already lifted in the Spirit.
The trumpet is already sounding through global events.
The next step is appearance.

6. Typology — Ensign = Covenant; Trumpet = Judgment; Mountain = Kingdom.

One verse contains the entire architecture of the end.

7. Technology — Heaven's Communications Network Is Open.

Signals are being sent.
Nations are receiving downloads they do not understand.
Prophets do.

MODE 3 — SPOKEN

*(What God is saying **now** to this generation)*

1. Spiritology — "Lift your eyes. The Banner is already raised."

Christ is signaling from Zion.
Not future — present.

2. Soulogy — "Stop waiting for signs. You are living in one."

The trumpet is not coming; it is already blowing through the crises of nations.

3. Physiology — "Prepare your body for glory alignment."

The remnant must live awakened, clean, responsive.

4. Theology — "My Kingdom is announcing its approach."

We are no longer in the age of speculation.
We are in the age of manifestation.

5. Chronology — "The generations have reached their convergence."

Everything is on schedule.
The return of the Lord is on the horizon of the age.

6. Typology — "As lightning lights the sky, so shall the Son of Man appear."

Isaiah 18:3 is the pressure wave before that flash.

7. Technology — "The global alert is active. My trumpet is sounding."

Heaven has moved from warning to summoning.

Prophetic Summation of Precept 5

Isaiah 18:3 is a global directive, not a local message.
The ensign = Christ revealed.
The trumpet = global spiritual wake-up call.
The mountains = the realms of divine government now rising.
All nations are under a single summons: **See. Hear. Prepare.**
The age is transitioning from the testimony of Christ to the appearance of Christ.

FINAL CRY OF ALIGNMENT

Even so, Lord Jesus, come quickly.
The banner is lifted.
The trumpet is sounding.
The Bride is awakening.
The nations are trembling.
The King is rising.

MATTHEW 24:2

2 And Jesus said unto them, See ye not all these things? verily I say unto you, There shall not be left here one stone upon another, that shall not be thrown down.

This is the demolition order of the kingdom. The Refiner does not negotiate with structures built in pride. Before He returns, everything that cannot carry the weight of His glory must fall.

MODE 1 — VISION

(What the Spirit is showing)

1. Spiritology — The Shaking Begins at the House of God.

In the Spirit, every false altar is already cracking. God permits no mixture in the place where His glory is destined to dwell.

2. Soulogy — Collective Disillusionment Has Begun.

People feel it:
The icons are failing.
The structures are hollow.
Systems cannot hold the future.

This is mercy masquerading as collapse.

3. Physiology — The Earth Responds to Unseen Commands.

Shifts in nature mirror shifts in heaven.

The physical world bends under spiritual pressure.

4. Theology — Jesus Pronounces a Non-Negotiable Judgment.

This is not advisory.
This is decree.
Human religion must bow to divine rule.

5. Chronology — We Are in the Pre-Fall, Pre-Build Stage.

Stage 1: Identification of false structures
Stage 2: Inevitable collapse
Stage 3: Raising of the eternal temple in the Spirit
We are already between Stage 1 and Stage 2.

6. Typology — As the Temple Fell in AD 70, So the Systems Fall Before His Return.

One is historical.
One is prophetic.
Both point to the same outcome:
the end of human glory, the rise of divine governance.

7. Technology — Heaven Has Initiated a Global Reset Protocol.

This is a top-down mandate:
If it's built by flesh, it must fall.
If it's built by the Spirit, it will rise.

MODE 2 — WRITTEN

(What the Scripture establishes in its structure)

1. Spiritology — "See Ye Not...?" Is a Command to Discern.

Jesus wasn't asking; He was requiring.
Discernment is the frontline technology of the final generation.

2. Soulogy — Human Expectations Must Collapse.

We cannot cling to things Christ commands to fall.

He removes the old so the Spirit may establish the new.

3. Physiology — Stones = Bodies, Structures, Institutions.

Every temple built without the Spirit's signature will not survive the shaking.

4. Theology — Christ Is Both Judge and Builder.

He tears down what is false, to raise what is true.

5. Chronology — This Verse Is the Trigger Mechanism for the End-Time Clock.

When earthly systems fall, the heavenly kingdom manifests.

6. Typology — Old Temple Down → New Temple Within Raised.

"Not one stone left" = Every prideful system dismantled.
"Temple rebuilt" = The remnant becoming the living stones of Zion.

7. Technology — The Word Is a Diagnostic Tool Revealing Corrupted Foundations.

Scripture scans the age, identifies architectural failure,
and announces divine renovation.

MODE 3 — SPOKEN

(What the Lord is saying right now to this generation)

1. Spiritology — "My glory will not inhabit polluted structures."

He is reclaiming His house.

2. Soulogy — "Detach from the things I am shaking."

Do not mourn the fall of systems that cannot steward His presence.

3. Physiology — "Your body is My temple — prepare it."

Holiness is not cosmetic; it is structural.

4. Theology — "The Cornerstone is returning; alignment is mandatory."

Before Christ appears, everything must realign around Him.

5. Chronology — "The countdown is active; the shaking intensifies."

The collapse is not the end; it is the clearing of the site for glory.

6. Typology — "As I tore down the temple, so I will tear down every throne of man."

Only the mountain of the Lord will stand.

7. Technology — "My trumpet is sounding through the fall of systems."

Economic systems, political structures, religious empires; these are the megaphones of prophecy.

The shaking is the announcement.

Prophetic Summation of Precept 6

Christ has issued a demolition command on all man-made systems.
The fall is not failure; it is preparation for glory.
This precept is the audit notice of history.
We are living in the seismic window before the unveiling of the Son.
The Spirit is relocating His dwelling into purified people, not structures.
This is the era of the living temple, the Spirit-filled Body, the remnant aligned with Zion.

FINAL ALIGNMENT DECLARATION

The stones are falling.
The thrones are trembling.
The Kingdom is rising.
The Bride is awakening.
The Spirit is speaking.

Even so, Lord Jesus, come quickly.

PRAYER

for Nationalisation into the Kingdom of Heaven

Scriptural Foundation:

- *John 3:3 – "Jesus answered and said to him, 'Most assuredly, I say to you, unless one is born again, he cannot see the kingdom of God.'"*

- *Philippians 3:20 – "For our citizenship is in heaven, from which we also eagerly wait for the Savior, the Lord Jesus Christ."*

- *Ephesians 2:19 – "Now therefore you are no longer strangers and foreigners, but fellow citizens with the saints and members of the household of God."*

- *Colossians 1:13 – "He has delivered us from the power of darkness and conveyed us into the kingdom of the Son of His love."*

- *Romans 10:9 – "That if you confess with your mouth the Lord Jesus and believe in your heart that God has raised Him from the dead, you will be saved."*

Righteous Judge of Heaven and Earth,

I come before Your throne, the **throne of Grace** in **the Court of Heaven**, in the name of Jesus Christ, my Lord and Saviour. I stand by the power of His precious blood, which has **redeemed me** and **bought my salvation**. I come humbly and boldly, desiring to be **nationalised into the Kingdom of Heaven**—to become a **true citizen of Your heavenly realm.**

Father, Your Word declares in **John 3:3** that **unless one is born again**, they cannot see the Kingdom of God. Today, **I renounce any citizenship** I once held in this world and any **ties to the powers of darkness**. I acknowledge that I have been **transferred from the kingdom of darkness into the Kingdom of the Son** of Your love (**_Colossians 1:13_**). I declare that I am no longer a stranger or foreigner, but a **fellow citizen with the saints** and a member of the household of God (**_Ephesians 2:19_**).

Lord Jesus, I believe with all my heart that You are the **Son of the living God**, that You died for my sins and rose again to grant me eternal life (**Romans 10:9**). I now receive You as my **personal Savior, my Redeemer, the only Way, the Truth**, and **the Life**. You are the **Door to the Father's heart** and the only **path to salvation**. I do not want to **perish** with the world, but to **live eternally with You**.

At this moment, I [Your Full Name] solemnly, sincerely, and truthfully affirm my love, my seriousness, and my desire to follow You and serve You in **holiness and righteousness**. I pledge my full allegiance to You, O King of kings and Lord of lords. I give my loyalty to the third Heaven and honour its **rights and freedoms**. I desire to settle with You, **Lord Jesus**. I repent of the way I have **lived my life and of all my sins**. Take over **my heart and my destiny**. Save me, cleanse me, and change me.

I beseech that You **seal my heavenly citizenship today**. Let the record of **my new identity** be **registered in the Court of Heaven**. Write my name in the **Lamb's Book of Life**, and erase it from the **book of death and judgment**. Let every **legal claim the enemy** has over my past be **cancelled** and **rendered powerless by the blood of Jesus**.

Lord, I am ready to walk the path of **righteousness and holiness**. I cast all **my cares and all of myself upon You**, for You care for me and loved me and laid Your life as the Lamb slain from **the foundation of the world**. Let Your **will be done** in my life as it is in Heaven.

By Your blood, I now receive eternal life. I proclaim that I am a **new creature**. By the word of Your testimony, I am made free indeed. **Fill me and baptize me** with the **Holy Ghost and fire**. Thank You, Lord Jesus, for giving me the right and the power to become a child of God, born **not of flesh but of the Spirit**, according to **the new covenant sealed in Your blood**.

I believe **You died** for me, and on the **third day**, You rose again. You are now seated at the right hand of the **Father in glory**, and I receive You as the Lord of my life. Through You, I have **received grace, peace, forgiveness, and eternal inheritance**. I stand holy, blameless, and without fault before the **Court of Heaven** because of the **righteousness imputed to me through Your sacrifice**.

Now, I **declare that the power of sin, death, and Satan—including the grave**—has been **broken over my life**. I walk in the eternal victory of the Cross. From this day forward, I will never look back. Backward—never. Forward—forever.

Degree and Declare: I am a citizen of Heaven. I live for Your Kingdom. **I walk in Your authority and power**. I receive the **full inheritance of health, peace, righteousness, Wealth, and provision, even eternal life**.

In Jesus' mighty name, I pray.

Amen.

EPILOGUE

The Spirit and the Bride Say, Come

(Revelation 22:17 KJV)

> *"And the Spirit and the bride say, Come.*
> *And let him that heareth say, Come.*
> *And let him that is athirst come.*
> *And whosoever will, let him take the water of life freely."*

The message now circles back to the beginning; the Voice that once walked in the garden calling, *"Where art thou?"* now thunders through eternity with a single invitation: **Come.**

Let the nations be warned.
Let the kings of the earth bow.
Let the idols of gold and pride crumble to dust.
Let every river of rebellion run dry before the flood of His glory.

Let the churches awaken.
For the hour is late, and the lamps grow dim.
The Bride must rise from slumber, trim her wick, and burn again with the first love.
The Spirit walks among the candlesticks, whispering to every heart that still listens:

"Cast off mixture. Return to the altar. The Bridegroom stands at the door."

And let Israel; the true sons of Spirit, not of flesh — return.
For the covenant still speaks.
The seed of Abraham is not bound by bloodline, but by obedience, those sealed with the mark of the Holy One in their inward parts.
The Father calls His firstborn from among the nations; a remnant chosen by grace, awakened by truth, purified in fire.

The heavens lean forward; the clock of eternity tolls its final beats.
Angels take their posts; the Lamb readies His procession.
The kingdoms of this world tremble as the scroll nears its last turning.
Creation itself holds its breath; for the Word that began all things is about to end them in glory.

The Spirit and the Bride say, Come.
This is not a whisper but a wave; a cry rolling from the hearts of the redeemed through every realm of existence.
It is the sound of alignment: Spirit and flesh joined in one voice.
The Bride no longer waits in uncertainty; she stands adorned, radiant, her garments washed in the blood of the Lamb, her lamp blazing with the oil of intimacy.

To the thirsty, the invitation stands: **Come.**
Not by merit, not by ritual, but by hunger.
For the water of life is freely given; a river clear as crystal, flowing from the throne and the Lamb.
All who come drink light; all who drink live forever.

And the One who testifies these things says again:

"Surely I come quickly."

The Bride answers; not in fear, but in fire:

"Even so, come, Lord Jesus."

The circle closes.
The mystery is complete.
Heaven and earth are one again.
The Sabbath has become the City.
The Word has returned to judge and to dwell.

And through all eternity, the song of the redeemed resounds:
Glory to the Lamb that was slain, for the kingdoms of this world have become the Kingdom of our God and of His Christ, and He shall reign forever and ever.

AFTERWORD

The final word echoes with the same fire as the first: **Jesus Christ is coming.**
Not as a distant rumour, not as a soft whisper in ancient pages, but as a living announcement moving through the earth at this very hour.

Across continents, across tribes, across the scattered sons of Israel, the message has gone forth.
Heaven has issued its brief.
The King has set His timetable.
The Spirit has sounded the internal alarm in the hearts of those who can still hear.

This book stands as a witness to that announcement.
Not the product of imagination, but the overflow of a message entrusted and delivered.
A stewardship.
A trumpet.
A signpost raised for a generation racing toward its appointed convergence with eternity.

If your heart stirred while reading these pages, consider it a gentle tap from the One who knocks.
If your spirit trembled at certain lines, consider it the wind of the Spirit aligning you with heaven's clock.
If your eyes opened to truths long hidden, consider it the hand of the Bridegroom preparing His own.

The mandate now is simple:

Return.
Awaken.
Stand ready.
Walk in the light of His appearing.

The hour is late, but grace still runs wide.
The nations shake, but His remnant stands secure.
The world grows darker, but the sons of Israel rise in the brightness of His glory.

And as these words close, one truth remains open forever:

"Surely I come quickly."
Even so, come, Lord Jesus.

ACKNOWLEDGEMENT

I extend my deepest gratitude to the One who authored this assignment—**Jesus Christ**, the Faithful and True Witness. Every insight, every scripture, every directive in this book originated from His voice. Without Him, there would be no message, no mandate, and no movement. He is the Source, the Strategy, and the Strength behind this work.

To the Holy Spirit, the Counselor who illuminates every truth and orchestrates every revelation, thank You for guiding each step with precision and grace. This message carries Your breath, Your fire, and Your signature of rest.

To the servants, intercessors, and prophetic witnesses across generations whose obedience kept the trail of truth alive, your sacrifices built the runway for this moment. Your faithfulness paved a path for this message to rise.

To the readers; those who approach this book with expectation, hunger, and humility, thank you. Your willingness to engage, to reflect, and to respond is the hinge on which transformation turns. Your journey matters. Your obedience moves Heaven.

To all who encouraged, prayed, supported, and believed while this message was being carried and shaped: you were the quiet scaffolding that strengthened the work until Christ's voice could stand on its own.

This book is dedicated upward, offered outward, and received forward. May its impact multiply. May its message return Israel to her Rest.

All honor to Jesus Christ—
the Sender, the Shepherd, and the Soon-Coming King.

ABOUT THE AUTHOR

Anthony Mwangi

Anthony Mwangi is a servant of Jesus Christ, called and commissioned to speak with clarity in a generation clouded by noise. His mandate is simple yet strategic: restore the ancient paths, unveil the hidden precepts, and prepare Israel, both scattered and sleeping, for the return of the King.

Operating as a prophetic teacher, Anthony carries a unique assignment rooted in Scripture, spiritual intelligence, and the 7-Dimensional Word of God. His work integrates Spirit, soul, and body with history, identity, and destiny, forming a comprehensive framework for believers who long to move from confusion into alignment.

Anthony is known for unveiling deep mysteries of Sabbath identity, spiritual warfare, prophetic chronology, and the original covenant DNA of God's people. His teachings are not drawn from ambition; they are received through vision, spoken instruction, and written revelation from Jesus Christ Himself.

Driven by purpose and anchored by obedience, Anthony stands as a witness to the urgency of the hour. His mission is not popularity; it is preparation. Not applause; but alignment. Not theory; but transformation.

This book represents one assignment among many; a forward-facing call to a world on the edge of the return of Christ.
A call to return.
A call to remember.
A call to rise.

All by the grace of Jesus Christ, the Author and Finisher of every faithful servant's journey.

BOOKS BY THIS AUTHOR

The Armour Of Light: Unlocking The Mystery Of Divine Warfare

In the last days, the battlefield is no longer fought with swords and spears, but with light, truth, and the Spirit. The Armour of Light: Unlocking the Mystery of Divine Warfare is a prophetic unveiling of God's end-time strategy for His chosen remnant.

This masterpiece reveals the hidden dimensions of the Word of God and the power of the Holy Spirit as the true armour that clothes, protects, and empowers the believer. Through spiritology, soulogy, physiology, and theology, the mystery of warfare is unfolded—showing how the Sabbath is God's dwelling place, the Courtroom of Heaven is His battlefield, and the Bride is His warrior.

Drawing from ancient truths and prophetic revelations, Anthony Mwangi — the BRANCH seated in Zion — uncovers the role of man in God's eternal judgment, the secret of Christ's blood as the light of warfare, and the revelation of the 7-dimensional Word as the weapon that disarms the dragon, the beast, and the false prophet.

This book is not just a teaching, but a weapon in itself. It equips the end-time believer to stand clothed in fire, sealed by the Spirit, and ready to triumph in the last battle.

If you are called to be part of the remnant, this is your manual of divine warfare.

Stars From The East (Irathiro)

The Scroll of Irathiro: The Rising Light from the East
By Anthony Mwangi — The BRANCH Seated in Zion

From the snows of Mount Kenya to the throne of eternal fire, The Scroll of Irathiro unveils a prophetic revelation hidden for generations. This masterpiece carries the light of divine remembrance — a message to restore identity, awaken the remnant, and call nations back to covenant truth.

Through the 7-Dimensional Word of God and the Spirit's rhythm of revelation, the author unfolds mysteries connecting ancient prophecy, African identity, and the returning glory of Christ — the King whose hair is white as wool and whose eyes burn with eternal purpose.

Each chapter breathes with vision and fire: from the golden offerings of the Magi to the judgment of nations, from the altar of Zion to the rivers of counsel flowing from the throne. It is not merely a book — it is a scroll of destiny, written in light and sealed in blood.

Those who read will find themselves within the story of restoration — called to stand as witnesses in the Court of Heaven, bearing the sign of the covenant and the song of the East.

Prophetic. Powerful. Undiluted truth.
This is not history retold — it is prophecy fulfilled.

The True Church (Ekklesia): The Undisputed Government Of Heaven On Earth

The Church was never designed to be a passive audience. It was crafted to be a governing body; Heaven's operational command centre on the earth.

This prophetic masterpiece unveils the Church in her original mandate: a ruling, legislative, fire-crowned government seated in Christ, built to administer righteousness, execute divine justice, and steward the expansion of the Kingdom with unshakeable authority.

Moving beyond institutional religion, this book repositions the reader inside the architectural blueprint of God's eternal design, where the Ekklesia stands as Heaven's governing senate, the Lamb's undefeated Heavyweight Government operating in light, truth, and dominion.

Each chapter pulls you deeper into the designer realm of the Word, where identity becomes structure and revelation becomes strategy. You will discover:

The true governmental nature of the Church
How sons legislate from Zion through rest, not striving
Why hell cannot contend with a people aligned to the Throne
How the 7-Dimensional Word of God equips believers for rule
The rise of Kingdom coalitions, watchtowers, and councils
The architecture of divine order that establishes peace without end
This is not just a teaching; it is a governmental activation. A call to rise, build, legislate, and stand in your ordained post within Heaven's expanding Kingdom.

For reformers, intercessors, apostolic builders, prophetic architects, and every believer hungry to move beyond survival into governance, this book is your blueprint.

Step into the council.
Stand in the light.

Take your seat in the Undisputed Government of the Lamb.

The Issue Of The Horse: The Courtroom Indictment Against Easter, Christmas, And Modern Pagan Feasts

In a generation reshaped by convenience, tradition, and cultural drift, what if the greatest spiritual compromise is hiding in plain sight?

This book issues a bold, courtroom-level challenge to the most celebrated religious holidays: Easter, Christmas, and the modern feasts that carry the fingerprints of Babylon more than the signature of God.

Drawing from prophetic insight, forensic Scripture analysis, and the ancient protocols of the Holy Spirit, The Issue of the Horse unmasks the systems that led believers away from covenant identity and into ritual mixtures dressed as worship. It reveals how syncretism infiltrated the church, how altars were exchanged, and why heaven's court is calling for a return to purity.

This is not a rant. It's a verdict.
A clear, uncompromising case built line upon line—rooted in the King James Bible, reinforced by historical evidence, and charged with a future-focused mandate: to realign the body of Christ with the original statutes of the Spirit.

Readers will discover:

The prophetic meaning of "the horse" and how it exposes counterfeit worship

Why certain feasts carry a spiritual indictment

How the courtroom of heaven evaluates worship, sacrifice, and alignment

The clash between the Holy Spirit's Sabbath identity and modern religious tradition

The call of Zion for believers to return to covenant rest and Spirit-governed truth

This book is a wake-up call for believers, leaders, intercessors, and truth-seekers who know something is off but have lacked the language, evidence, and prophetic clarity to name it.

If you're ready to confront the mixture, reclaim ancient order, and stand in the firelight of truth,step into the courtroom.
The Spirit has issued a summons.
The verdict is unfolding.
And the remnant is rising.

Sabbath: The Name Of The Holy Spirit — God's Covenant Protocol For The Last Days

This book unveils a groundbreaking revelation: the Sabbath is the Name, Seal, and Rest of the Holy Spirit, and the end-time Church cannot walk in covenant power without understanding this identity. Drawing from the 7-Dimensional Word of God, this work decodes the Sabbath as God's ancient–future protocol — the original sign of His presence, the governing code of His kingdom, and the prophetic mark that distinguishes His remnant in the last days.

You will discover how the Sabbath reveals God's hidden Name, aligns the mind with divine order, and positions the body as the dwelling place where the Spirit rests. From Eden's first seventh-day revelation to the sealed remnant of Revelation, this book demonstrates that to hallow the Sabbath is to hallow His Name, and that the restoration of Sabbath order is the restoration of God's government on earth.

Packed with visionary insights, prophetic typology, and a full blueprint for spiritual formation, this book equips believers to:

Understand the Sabbath as the signature identity of the Holy Spirit

Discern the covenant seal that separates truth from deception in the last days

Rebuild the altar of rest in the mind, heart, and body

Walk in the rhythm, protection, and judgment of God's kingdom order

Stand in Zion as those who have entered His Rest

This is not merely theology — it is kingdom strategy.
A call to return.
A summons to alignment.
A preparation for the remnant.

SABBATH: The Name of the Holy Spirit is your guide to reclaiming God's original covenant protocol, and stepping into the Rest that marks His people for the final generation.

Deliverance By Fire: Unlocking The Courts, Thrones, And Altars Of True Freedom

This prophetic manual is not just a teaching — it is a spiritual courtroom, an altar of judgment, and a throne of fire. Deliverance by Fire unveils the divine order of freedom as legislated in heaven's courts and manifested through the Spirit of Truth on earth.

Within these pages, you will encounter the architecture of true deliverance:
the Courts of Heaven, where accusations are silenced;
the Thrones of Dominion, where believers reign in Christ;
and the Altars of Fire, where covenants are purified and destinies reborn.

Built upon the revelation of the Seven Spirits of God, this book exposes the counterfeit thrones of darkness — and trains the sons and daughters of Zion to war by decree, not emotion; by the Word, not the flesh. Each chapter blends courtroom insight, prophetic instruction, and altar-based declarations to forge warriors of holiness and rest.

Through this 7-dimensional model — Spiritology, Soulogy, Physiology, Theology, Chronology, Typology, and Technology — Anthony Mwangi reveals how the Spirit of Judgment and Burning restores divine order, purges bloodlines, and reclaims the altars of families, cities, and nations.

This book will teach you to:

Minister deliverance through heavenly legal protocol.

Break bloodline covenants and generational curses with the fire of truth.

Build Sabbath altars that sustain freedom and spiritual authority.

Operate in the courts of Zion, where Christ is both Judge and Advocate.

Move from manifestation to dominion — from reaction to legislation.

Deliverance by Fire is more than deliverance — it is reformation. It is the blueprint of how heaven reclaims the earth through purified vessels who have become living stones and burning altars of the Spirit.

When you finish reading, you will not just understand deliverance —

you will embody it.

READER ACTIVATION

"The Return Mandate"

As you close this book,
you are not closing the message.
You are stepping into an assignment.

Your mandate is threefold:

1. Return to the Lord

Not halfway.
Not casually.
With your whole heart, soul, and strength.

2. Awaken Others

Share what you have received.
Blow the trumpet.
Lift the banner.
Call the scattered ones to the Shepherd of Israel.

3. Stand in Readiness

Watch.
Pray.
Discern the times.
Let your life carry the gravity of a prophetic generation
that knows the King is at the door.

FINAL CHARGE

"Until He Appears in Glory"

Step forward with holy confidence.
Walk as one marked by revelation.
Let your decisions reflect the nearness of eternity.
Carry yourself as part of the company chosen to announce His return.

You are not reading history
you are stepping into prophecy.
You are not waiting for a distant hope
you are aligning with heaven's present movement.

Let the fire in your spirit stay lit.
Let the urgency of Christ's message guide your days.
Let your voice be one of the many rising across the earth, saying:

"Prepare the way for the King of Glory."

And when the last trumpet sounds,
and the heavens open,
may you be found ready; awake, faithful, and standing.

CLOSING PRAYER

"Seal Us for Your Coming"

Lord Jesus Christ,
You who walk among the lamps of heaven,
You who speak with a voice like many waters,
Let this message be sealed in the spirits of all who read it.

Awaken every slumbering heart.
Realign every wandering soul.
Restore every fractured identity.
Gather Your scattered sons and daughters from the ends of the earth.

Plant the fear of the LORD within us.
Clothe us with readiness.
Mark us with the oil of the Spirit.
Strengthen us to stand in the day of Your appearing.

And until the skies split with Your glory,
Keep us faithful, steadfast, unmovable—
A people prepared for the King.

Amen.
Even so, Lord Jesus, come.

www.ingramcontent.com/pod-product-compliance
Lightning Source LLC
Chambersburg PA
CBHW071608040426
42452CB00008B/1277